VIKING
INSTAGRAM INFLUENCERS

Viking_Reviews

DogByts

10/10

LIKES : 10.356.586

Viking_Reviews Guys you need to try...

Chapter 1:

Intro to Instagram Influencers

In the golden age of social media, every business has at least one online account. For most businesses, Facebook and Twitter are probably the go-to social media platforms when creating an online presence. However, this means that Instagram, the world's fastest growing social media app, is being overlooked. Instagram currently has more than 800 million monthly users with an average 3.21% user engagement rate, more than double the average social media rate of 1.5%.

90% of the one hundred most popular brands are on Instagram, 70% of the most-used hashtags on social media feature brands and 50% of Instagram users use the app to research products. How did this all happen? How did Instagram, a social media platform, become such a highly-trusted source for product and brand information? In a word, influencers.

There are influencers on pretty much every social media platform, with Instagram, YouTube, and Twitter being the most prevalent. An influencer is someone with a large sphere of influence; this term includes celebrities, but is usually reserved for people who have built their personal brand almost exclusively on social media.

Instagram users are more likely to connect with influencers than celebrities because they seem more "normal"- usually because they post about their life, food, and pets on a daily basis. Influencers are often seen as the middle ground between the average Joe and a celebrity- they have glamorous holidays and beautiful selfies, but they don't live in LA or drive a Ferrari. Social media users like and trust influencers because they see their status as attainable- once upon a time, each influencer was just like them. Many Instagram users try to emulate influencers in the hope of gaining their own influence. As they do that, they look to influencers' posts for inspiration and guidance, eagerly absorbing any marketing messages those posts may contain.

A company working with an Instagram influencer pays the influencer to include their product or service in a post. This includes tagging the company's Instagram (if they have one) in the photo and in the post description. The post usually features a photo of the influencer using the product and a description of why they like it. Sponsored posts can often just feature an aesthetically pleasing photo of the product, as this is also a large part of Instagram culture.

What kind of product or service your company sells will inform your decision of which influencer you work with. The most popular Instagram influencers break down into three categories: celebrities, fitness, and beauty. The "celebrities" category features people who are famous outside of Instagram and other social media- singers, actors, etc. These users do make featured posts, but they are very expensive to hire and tend to only work with large brands. For most companies, it's best to focus on the traditional Instagram influencer- someone whose fame and influence is exclusive to social media. Fitness influencers tend to promote gyms, exercise equipment, sportswear brands, and healthy food and drink products. Beauty influencers tend to promote makeup, skincare, fashion, and homeware products. Many influencers, regardless of their profile's style, will also promote "lifestyle" products such as vacation services and clothes. Instagram is about presenting a curated version of your lifestyle to your followers, so you'll want to collaborate with an influencer whose lifestyle fits your product.

Working with an Instagram influencer can help to boost awareness of your brand and show your product being used by someone your potential customers admire. Many Instagram users follow influencers because they share their interests. Therefore, if a user sees an influencer using and enjoying your product, they're more likely to think they'd enjoy using it too. Having an influencer feature your product on their account shows customers what your product is, how it can be used, and where to find it. Instagram advertising can be even more effective than traditional ads because it can really capture the joy a user gets from a product they love.

Chapter 2:

What to Look for in Influencers

When looking for an influencer to collaborate with, you might be tempted to simply go with whoever has the highest follower count. After all, more followers means more ad views, right? Not necessarily. Here's a breakdown of what you should be looking for when searching for an influencer to collaborate with:

Budget

Rates for a sponsored post on an influencer's account can vary wildly according to their popularity. You can spend as little as $100 on a post by someone with less than five thousand followers, or over $500,000 on a post by a top Instagram user like Selena Gomez or Kim Kardashian. Decide what your budget is, and search for an influencer within that range. Many Instagram influencers have signed up with agencies that pair them with brands looking to sponsor posts, which can also help you find an influencer to suit your brand.

Right demographic

Consider the age, gender(s), and interests of the people you want to attract. While you may initially think that only teenagers and young adults use Instagram, this is far from true. Instagram users tend to follow influencers who emulate them, so look for someone who represents your key demographic. For example, if you want to promote your brand to sporty men in their early thirties, look at sporty male influencers in their early thirties. You can also use a range of Instagram analysis and marketing sites that will tell you which accounts have the most followers within your preferred demographic.

Right kind of profile

Again, the influencer you work with needs to match the customers you're trying to reach. Working with a fitness Instagrammer to promote your new burger restaurant probably won't be very effective. Find an influencer who would conceivably enjoy your product- they'll be able to sell it best.

High engagement rate

While Instagram has a higher engagement rate than other social media platforms, this rate isn't the same for all accounts. Interestingly, studies have shown that the more followers an Instagram account has, the lower its user engagement rate. This means that if you really want users to engage with your product, you should work with someone who has ten thousand followers instead of ten million.

Follower count

Despite the high follower/low engagement trend, you don't want to sponsor an influencer with a small sphere of influence. Influencers with less than five thousand followers have the highest engagement rate at 8%, but 8% of five thousand is only four hundred users. In contrast, influencers with up to 100,000 followers tend to only have a 2.4% engagement rate, but 2.4% of 100,000 is 2,400 users. When examining your options for an Instagram collaborator, it's best to measure each user's engagement rate against their follower count to calculate exactly how many people you can reach.

Chapter 3:

Working with Influencers

Now you know what an influencer is and how they work, but how exactly do you work with them? Well, it's really up to you. Depending on what the influencer is willing to do, you have a few options.

The most popular choice for sponsored content is a single post. This includes your product featured in a photo with your company's account tagged in the photo and description. Many influencers will work with brands more than once, and can feature your product in multiple posts over a time frame of your choosing. How you schedule this depends on whether you want to build momentum for an upcoming launch or announce multiple launches.

For example, if launching a single product, you may choose to sponsor three posts over a month. You could give the influencer the product before general release and have them share their thoughts with their followers. If you are launching a range, it could be helpful to have individual posts for each product and another for the entire range together.

One of Instagram's more recent features, stories, is also a great place to buy sponsored content. Instagram stories are a series of photos and videos put up by the user that only exist for 24 hours. These photos and videos can have text, emojis, and effects added to give the story a more fun, casual feel.

Whenever an influencer creates sponsored content for you, they should use appropriate hashtags and tag your profile. Feel free to give the influencer the exact hashtags you want to use- using the same hashtags on your own profile will mean that both profiles show up when a user clicks the hashtag.

Many brands will give the influencer the copy they want in the post's description, word for word. You can discuss with the influencer whether you want to do this or let them voice their opinions.

As you can imagine, one post is cheaper than multiple posts. An influencer's rate will depend on their follower count and user engagement rate. Generally speaking, you can expect a post to cost about three times as much as a story. Many influencers who work with brands will have deals for multiple posts- for example, they may have a discounted rate for three or five posts within a month.

You can also work with more than one influencer at a time. Many brands do this by sending out a new product to multiple influencers on release and asking them to review it. Because influencers with lower follower counts have a higher engagement rate, your ads could be seen by more people if you work with two smaller influencers rather than one bigger one. Working with multiple influencers also allows you to advertise to multiple demographics. Your product might have a wider appeal than one individual, so diversifying your collaborations will give you a wider reach.

Mentioning an influencer's review or post about your product on your own Instagram account will draw attention to that post and cause it to be given higher priority by Instagram's algorithms. Instagram features popular posts more prominently, so giving your sponsored post a shout-out will help it to be seen by even more people. Mentioning the influencer will also create a relationship between the person and your brand, creating a sense of friendship and personality that customers will appreciate.

Conclusion

Now that you're Instagram-savvy, it's time to go out and use your influence! You can use your new knowledge to find the perfect influencer for your brand and collaborate on content that will have users rushing to their online shopping carts. Before you go, let's look over a few key facts:

An influencer's appeal comes from their glamorous yet attainable lifestyle. They share details of their everyday life but intersperse their posts with glamorous products. By featuring your brand, the influencer is showing their followers that they can achieve this same glamorous lifestyle with your products.

There are multiple categories of Instagram influencers, the most popular being fitness, beauty, and lifestyle. Think about which category suits your product best, and work with influencers within that niche.

Quality, not quantity: follower count isn't always the most important factor when finding an influencer to work with. Instagram has shown that accounts with a higher follower count have a lower user engagement rate. You'll want to find that sweet spot where an influencer has a few thousand followers but still has a relatively high engagement rate.

Consider your sponsoring options: do you want your product featured in a post, a story, both, or even multiple posts and stories? Most influencers who agree to sponsored content will be open to all of these options, so it's up to you to decide what would work best for your brand (and budget).

If you haven't already, make sure to set up an Instagram account for your company before working with an influencer. This will allow anyone who is interested in their posts to easily find your products and follow you. You never know, a successful collaboration could do wonders for your own sphere of influence!

www.ingramcontent.com/pod-product-compliance
Lightning Source LLC
Chambersburg PA
CBRC090851210326
41597CB00011B/173